Plants That Eat Animals

Contents

Written by Sally Morgan

Collins

1 Introduction

All living things need food. Animals can't make their own food, so they eat other living things. Many animals eat plants, while some animals eat other animals.

Plants make their own food using sunlight. But there are some special plants that feed on small animals, like flies and spiders. These are called **carnivorous** plants.

You'll read about all sorts of carnivorous plants in this book, but they are all harmless to people and large animals.

a carnivorous plant

3

2 How plants make food

Plants have green leaves that grow towards the sun. They use sunlight and carbon dioxide to make sugars. Carbon dioxide is a gas in the air.

sunlight in

carbon dioxide in

Plants use the sugars to grow and **reproduce**. Sugars are moved around the plant to where they are needed. Some sugars go to make new leaves and flowers. Some go to the roots where they're stored as **starch**.

When they make sugars, plants produce a gas called oxygen. Animals need oxygen to breathe.

Plants don't just need sugars to stay healthy. They need other **nutrients** which their roots take up from the soil.

oxygen out

sugars

water and nutrients in

Some plants live in places where there aren't many nutrients in the soil. To stay healthy, they need to find another source of nutrients. They do this by feeding on animals.

Worldwide, there are more than a thousand different types of plants that eat animals. Many of these plants are found in **swamps** and boggy places. Swampy soils have lots of water, but few nutrients. Others are found on trees in tropical rainforests. Some live in water where they feed on tiny **aquatic** animals.

Plants can't move from place to place, so they have ways of attracting animals to them and trapping them.

a swamp

6

a rainforest

3 Sticky leaves and traps

Sundews are small plants that are found growing in boggy places. They produce a sticky glue to catch **prey**. Their leaves are covered in long sticky hairs. When you look closely, you can see a drop of glue at the end of each hair. It looks like a drop of water.

sundew

An insect landing on a sundew leaf gets stuck. It can't escape. Slowly, the leaf wraps around the insect and it dies. Sundews feed mostly on small insects like flies, but they trap spiders too. Sometimes, larger insects get trapped when their wings touch the glue.

Butterworts have sticky leaves just like sundews. They are small plants with bright green leaves in the shape of a triangle. Any small insect landing on a sticky leaf gets trapped. Slowly, the leaves roll up around the insect and it can't escape.

The Victorians used to grow pots of butterworts in their greenhouses. Their leaves trapped many small whiteflies that would eat their other plants.

Butterwort leaves were once used in cheesemaking. To make cheese, milk has to be **curdled** so it forms lumps. The lumps are separated from the liquid milk and made into cheese. In the past, people dropped butterwort leaves into milk to help it curdle.

butterwort

Another plant that catches flies is the Venus flytrap.
It grows in the swamps in North America where there are
lots of flies.

Their leaves snap shut like a trap! Each leaf is formed
from two parts which are joined together in the middle.
The inside of the leaf is bright red and there's a row of
spines along the edge. It looks like a big mouth.

Venus flytrap

When the leaf is open, flies see the red colour. They think it's a flower and land on the leaf. As soon as a fly touches a spine, the leaf snaps shut. The fly is trapped and is unable to escape.

4 Pitcher plants

Pitcher plants have a different way of catching their prey. They get their name from the way their leaves are shaped like jugs, called pitchers, and contain water. Most have a lid too. Some pitcher plants hang from trees. Others grow on the ground.

lid

Flies and spiders are attracted to the pitchers by their sweet smell. But the walls of the pitcher are slippery. When the insects crawl inside to find food, they slip into the water. They can't get out and they **drown** in the water.

Some pitchers are huge and can trap animals like frogs and rats.

An interesting pitcher plant is the cobra lily. It looks just like a cobra, a type of snake. Its pitchers are shaped like a tube with a hood at the top. The two petal-like leaves under the hood look just like the forked tongue of a snake. There's lots of **nectar** on the "tongue" which **lures** insects into the pitcher. Insects squeeze through the tiny entrance. But once they are inside, they can't get out because the entrance is blocked by downward pointing hairs, and they slip down into the water.

cobra

5 Toilet pitcher plants

Some pitcher plants don't trap animals but obtain the nutrients they require to grow from animal waste instead.

Toilet pitcher plants have large pitchers that are the size of a small football. They produce lots of sweet nectar to attract animals, such as birds, squirrels, rats and tree shrews. They don't eat these animals. Instead, the animals sit on the top of the pitcher and lick nectar off the lid. As they do this, they go to the toilet and the plants use the nutrients in the waste.

bat

Some small bats **roost** in pitcher plants. They creep inside the pitcher to shelter from the rain. While they rest, they go to the toilet in the pitcher.

tree shrew

6 Water plants

The bladderwort is an aquatic plant. It lives in water and catches animals with its suction trap.

The bladderwort has a long stem that floats in water. Along the stem are traps or **bladders**, which look like tiny bags. When a water animal touches one of the hairs around the bladder, the bladder **expands**. This sucks water into the bladder, carrying the animal with it.
This happens in a fraction of a second.
The bladder returns to its original size
and squashes the animal.
Then the bladder is ready to
trap another animal.

bladderwort

Waterwheel plants are aquatic too. They feed on tiny water animals, such as water fleas.

At first sight, a waterwheel plant looks like any other waterweed, with a stem and **whorls** of leaves. But look closely and you see the leaves are tiny traps. Each trap is formed from two parts joined together, just like the snap trap of the Venus flytrap. The trap has lots of long hairs. Once a water animal touches a hair, the trap snaps shut, and the animal is trapped.

waterwheel plant

waterwheel plant catching its prey

7 Keeping a carnivorous plant

If you've been fascinated by carnivorous plants, you could grow one at home. One of the easiest to grow is the Venus flytrap. Keep it near a window so it gets lots of light, but make sure it doesn't get too hot in summer. It doesn't like garden soil, so you should buy a special compost with the right mix of ingredients.

There are many other carnivorous plants you could grow at home, including sundews, butterworts and even pitcher plants. You could keep them in a greenhouse to help to keep down the number of insects feeding on the plants.

So what have you discovered about carnivorous plants? Carnivorous plants have clever ways of getting the nutrients they require by trapping animals. Some have sticky hairs, others have leaves that snap shut, or are shaped like pitchers. They grow in forests, swamps, bogs and even in streams and ponds.

These are weird and wonderful plants that eat other living things, but don't harm us.

Glossary

aquatic living in water

bladders bag-like structures

carnivorous feeding on animals

curdled when lumps have formed in liquids

drown to die from lack of air under water

expands gets larger

lures tempts an animal or person to do something

nectar a sweet liquid produced by plants to attract animals

nutrients substances that are essential for health

prey an animal that is hunted by others

reproduce to produce babies

roost to rest

starch a type of food found in potatoes and bread

swamps low-lying places with lots of water

whorls circles of leaves around a stem

Index

Plants that eat animals

Name of plant		
sundew, butterwort	pitcher plants	toilet pitcher plants
How they catch their prey		
sticky leaves	jug-shaped leaves filled with water – flies and other small animals slip into the water and drown	catch animal waste
Picture		

cobra lily	Venus flytrap	bladderworts, waterwheel plants
use their pitcher to trap insects	leaves snap shut like a trap	suction traps and hairs to catch tiny animals

Ideas for reading

Written by Gill Matthews
Primary Literacy Consultant

Reading objectives:
- identify main ideas drawn from more than one paragraph and summarising these
- identify how language, structure, and presentation contribute to meaning
- retrieve and record information from non-fiction

Spoken language objectives:
- articulate and justify answers, arguments and opinions
- give well-structured descriptions, explanations and narratives for different purposes
- use spoken language to develop understanding through speculating, hypothesising, imagining and exploring ideas

Curriculum links: Science – Plants; Animals, including humans

Interest words: structures, tempts, produced, essential

Resources: IT, information books

Build a context for reading

- Explain to the children that the book they are going to read is called *Plants That Eat Animals*. Explore what the title means to them. Ask them to look at the photo on the front cover and discuss what they can see. Read the back-cover blurb and ask children what they think they will find out from the book.

- Establish that this is an information book. Ask children what kind of features they expect to find in the book. Give them time to scan the book to find the contents, glossary and index. Discuss the purpose and organisation of each of these features.

Understand and apply reading strategies

- Ask children to use the contents to find the chapter called *Introduction*. Read pp2–3 aloud. Ask why the word *carnivorous* is in bold. Give children time to find it in the glossary and explain what it means.

- Discuss what information the large photo on pp2–3 is supporting.